What's it like to be a...

RAILROAD WORKER

Written by Morgan Matthews
Illustrated by Lynn Sweat

Troll Associates

Special Consultant Group: New Jersey Transit Rail Operations,
Newark, New Jersey.

Library of Congress Cataloging-in-Publication Data

Matthews, Morgan.
    What's it like to be a railroad worker / by Morgan Matthews;
illustrated by Lynn Sweat.
        p.   cm.—(Young careers)
    Summary: Describes the jobs of a variety of people involved in
railroad work, including the conductor, engineer, and brakeman.
    ISBN 0-8167-1815-6 (lib. bdg.)   ISBN 0-8167-1816-4 (pbk.)
    1. Railroads—Employees—Juvenile literature. 2. Railroads—
Vocational guidance—Juvenile literature. [1. Railroads.
2. Occupations.] I. Sweat, Lynn, ill. II. Title. III. Series.
HD8039.R1M37 1990
385'.023'73—dc20
                                            89-34389

What's it like to be a...

RAILROAD WORKER

Whooo! Whooo!
"Listen!" says Jimmy.

The Johnson family is at the train station.
They are going on a trip. Jimmy is excited. He
has never been on a train before.

"Good! Our train is on time," says Mrs. Johnson.

Every train follows a special schedule, or plan. The schedule tells each place the train will go and when it will get there. Trains go from city to city and from state to state. Some even go from one country to another.

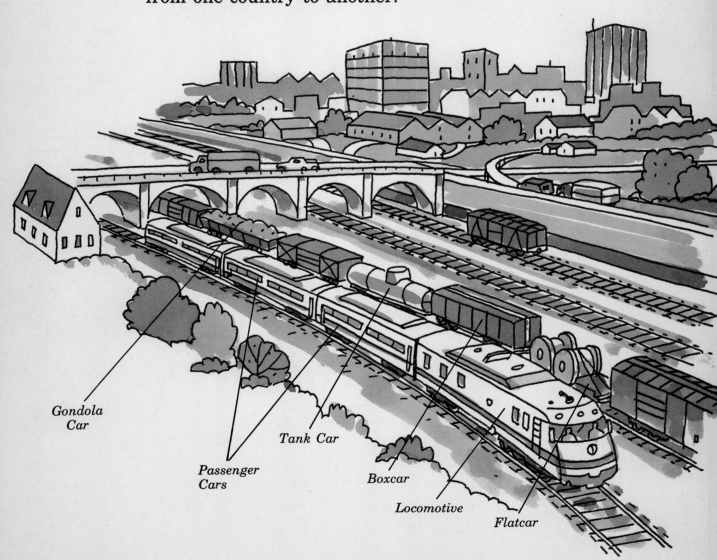

Gondola Car

Passenger Cars

Tank Car

Boxcar

Locomotive

Flatcar

The train comes slowly into the station. *Whoosh!* Air brakes screech. The train stops. It has many cars. In front is the sleek locomotive that pulls the train.

There are many kinds of locomotives. Long ago, steam locomotives burned wood or coal for fuel. Today, diesel locomotives use fuel oil. Modern electric locomotives travel very fast. Some can go over two hundred miles an hour.

Steam Locomotive

Smokestack

Headlight

Drive Wheel

Cowcatcher

Diesel Locomotive

Electric Passenger Car

Catenary

Pantograph

DINING CAR

Behind the locomotive are other cars. The dining car serves meals. Pullman cars have seats that can be made into beds. Jimmy's family will sleep in one of the Pullman cars tonight. Luggage and packages have been loaded into the baggage car.

"Time to board," says Mr. Johnson. Jimmy and his parents get on the train. Soon the train starts to move.

"Working on a train must be exciting," Jimmy says.

Jimmy's mom nods. "It takes many people to run a train," she says. "There is one of the most important people. He's the conductor."
Jimmy sees a man in a dark suit and cap.

The conductor knows all about trains. He is like the captain of a ship. A crew of people work on the train. The conductor tells each one what job to do.

The conductor does other jobs, too. He checks the train to make sure it is safe. On a passenger train like this one, he collects tickets from the riders.

"Tickets, please," the conductor says to Mr. Johnson. The conductor punches holes in the tickets, so they can't be used again.

"Do you ever drive the train?" asks Jimmy. The conductor smiles. "No, the engineer operates the train," he answers. "But many other people work to make each trip a smooth one!"

Whistle

Windshield Wiper

There are people who direct railroad traffic with flags or other signals. There are crews of workers who keep the tracks in good repair by replacing broken ties and rails.

Electric Wires (Catenary)

Headlight

Locomotive

Signal Light

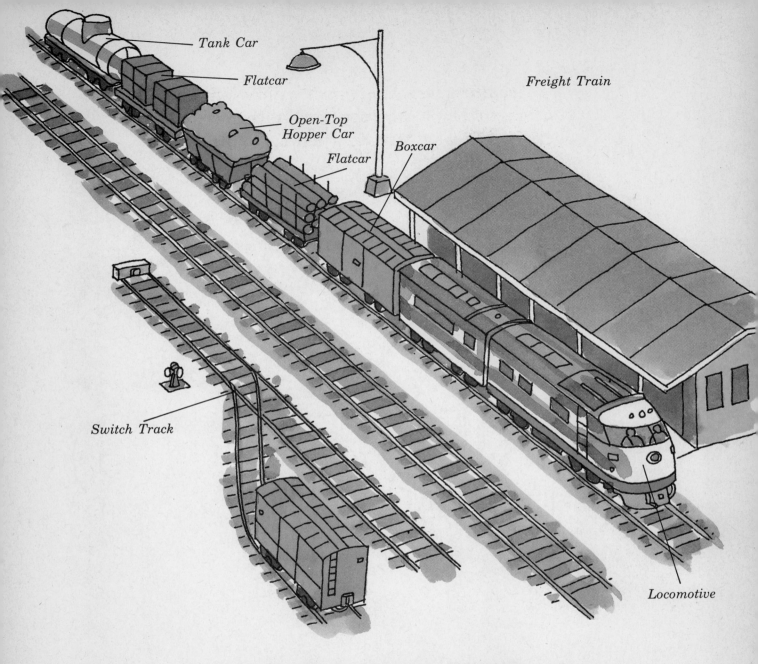

Tank Car

Flatcar

Open-Top
Hopper Car

Flatcar

Boxcar

Freight Train

Switch Track

Locomotive

There are people who work in freight yards,
loading and unloading the many different kinds
of cars on the long freight trains. Freight trains
carry all kinds of goods—oil, lumber, machinery,
and more.

An engineer has many responsibilities. He is in charge of the locomotive. Before each trip, he checks it to make sure it's running well.

Wayside Signal

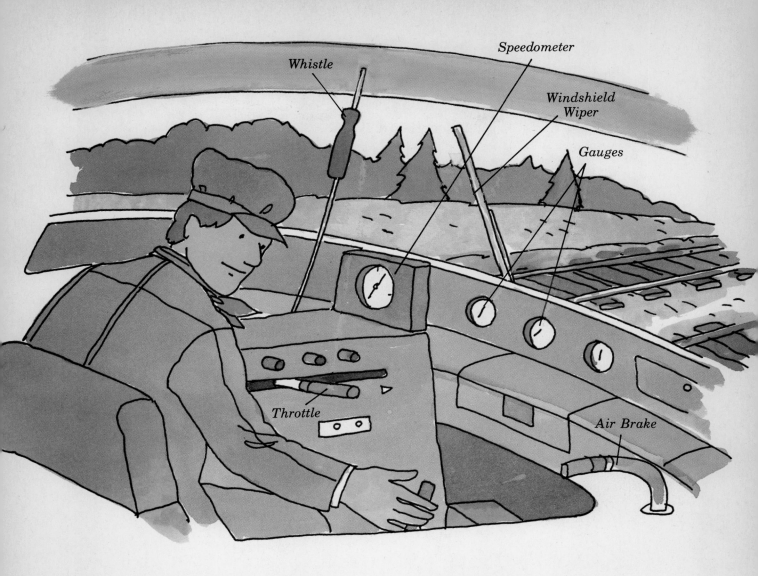

Whistle

Speedometer

Windshield Wiper

Gauges

Throttle

Air Brake

Driving a locomotive is not easy. The engineer must know how to handle many controls. A special handle, or lever, makes the train go forward or backward. The throttle makes it go fast or slow. The air brake is for stopping. There are dials and gauges for checking speed, pressure, and other things.

Most important, to operate the train safely, the engineer must know all railroad signs and signals.

"Good," says the engineer. "A clear signal. We can go fast."

The engineer drives the train in all kinds of weather. Trains can move on ice and snow. The engineer puts sand on an icy track by pulling a lever. Sometimes huge snowplows clear the tracks for the trains that will follow.

Snowplow

Even mountains and rivers do not stop trains. A train can travel through a long tunnel dug right into the side of a mountain. To cross a wide river, a train travels upon a high bridge. The engineer must be watchful and alert, as he guides the train along.

In the locomotive, the engineer has a helper. He is the fireman. His name comes from the days when steam locomotives were used. The fireman used to put wood or coal in the fire to keep the steam engine running.

The fireman's job is to watch the many gauges in the locomotive. He must also look out for anything blocking the track. The fireman is always ready to take over for the engineer in an emergency.

Signal Tower

Caboose

Switch Stand

Flagman

Signal Flag

A flagman usually rides at the back of the train. On a freight train, the last car is called the caboose. From the caboose, the flagman watches for trouble as the train moves.

Years ago, when the train stopped, the flag-man had to get out and stand by the tracks. He had to make sure another train did not run into his. If he saw a train coming, the flagman signaled the other train to stop with his lantern. Now signal lights are used for this important job.

Signal Light

Lantern

Ties

Rails

Porters and baggagemen help make the
passengers comfortable. They also help to carry
and load bundles and luggage onto the train.

"Look!" cries Jimmy.
A long train is passing on another track.
"It's a freight train," says the conductor.
Jimmy watches the many different freight
cars.

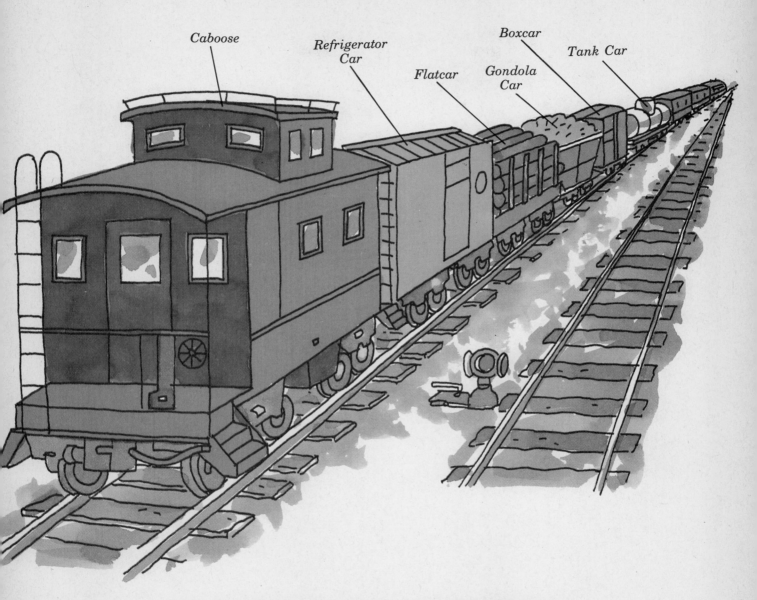

Caboose

Refrigerator Car

Flatcar

Gondola Car

Boxcar

Tank Car

Boxcars pass. There are flatcars and hopper cars filled with coal. Tank cars and refrigerator cars go by. There are gondolas filled with scrap metal.

"There's the caboose!" shouts Jimmy. "What a long train! I bet a lot of people worked to load all that freight."

The conductor smiles. "Yes, and a lot of other people help to keep the trains running, too. Special crews clean and repair tracks. Some railroad people work in stations. Others work in the yards, where the trains are kept. There are even trains called subways that run under cities."

Subway Train

Subway Platform

Jimmy watches the freight train disappear. "The job I like best is engineer," he says. "I'd like to run a locomotive."

The conductor laughs. "Someday maybe you will!"